Read and Do Science
WATER and ICE

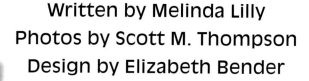

Written by Melinda Lilly
Photos by Scott M. Thompson
Design by Elizabeth Bender

Educational Consultants

Kimberly Weiner, Ed.D

Betty Carter, Ed.D

Maria Czech, Ph.D
California State University Northridge

Rourke
Publishing LLC
Vero Beach, Florida 32964

Before You Read This Book

Think about these facts:

1. What is ice made of?

2. Where does rain come from?

The experiments in this book should be undertaken with adult supervision.

For the Berry family

— S. T.

©2006 Rourke Publishing LLC

Photo Credits: page 4b, courtesy of the National Park Service; page 7 courtesy of the National Park Service; page 8, courtesy of National Oceanic and Atmospheric Administration (NOAA)/Department of Commerce, and Commander John Bortniak, NOAA Corps (ret.); page 11, courtesy of National Oceanic and Atmospheric Administration (NOAA)/Department of Commerce, and Captain Budd Christman, NOAA Corps; page 12b, courtesy of National Oceanic and Atmospheric Administration (NOAA)/Department of Commerce; page 13, courtesy of the National Park Service; page 23, courtesy of National Oceanic and Atmospheric Administration (NOAA)/Department of Commerce

Library of Congress Cataloging-in-Publication Data

Lilly, Melinda
  Water and Ice / Lilly, Melinda.
    p. cm. -- (Read and do science)
  ISBN 1-59515-406-X (hardcover)

Printed in the USA

Table of Contents

Ladies and Gentlemen, Boys and Girls... Water Can Perform Amazing Stunts!

It can disappear before your very eyes.

On a warm day, take water outside with you or find some nearby.

Wet your finger.

Write your name in water on a sidewalk. Watch as your name disappears!

5

What Happened to Your Name?

The sun heated the water and made it **evaporate.** The water became part of the air.

Poof!

It became **water vapor,** drops of water that are too small to see and float in the air. Water vapor is a **gas.** The water changed from a liquid to a gas.

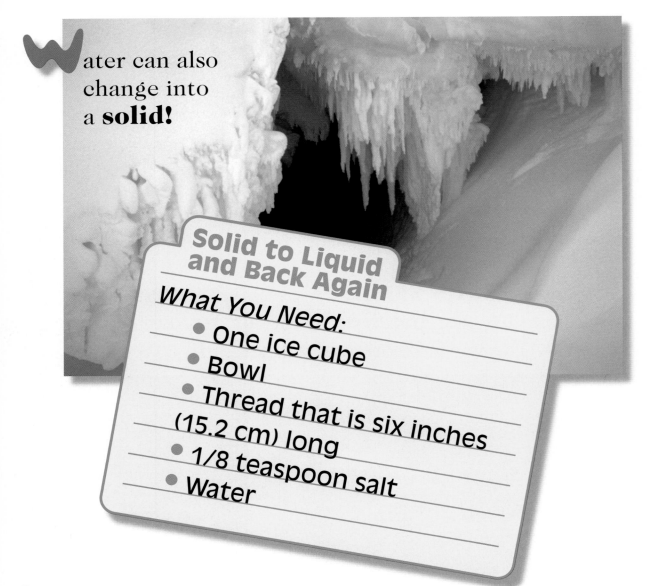

Water can also change into a **solid!**

Solid to Liquid and Back Again

What You Need:

- One ice cube
- Bowl
- Thread that is six inches (15.2 cm) long
- 1/8 teaspoon salt
- Water

Wet the ice cube or get it warm and . . .

Make it **melt**!

Set it in the bowl.

Lay the thread in a loop on the ice cube with the ends hanging off either side.

Sprinkle salt on the thread where it sits on the ice.

Count to thirty.

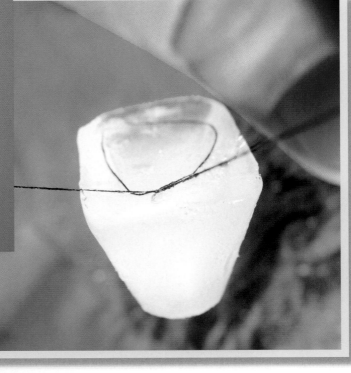

Wow!

Hold both ends of the thread and lift. The thread lifts the ice!

10

The Secret of Water, Ice, and Salt

ater freezes at 32 degrees Fahrenheit (0 degrees Celsius). Salt water freezes at a lower **temperature.** For example, the ocean begins to freeze at 28 degrees Fahrenheit (-2.2 degrees Celsius).

Come on in, the water's great!

When you sprinkled the salt, the ice melted slightly. The top of the ice turned from a solid into a liquid. However, the rest of the ice cube stayed cold.

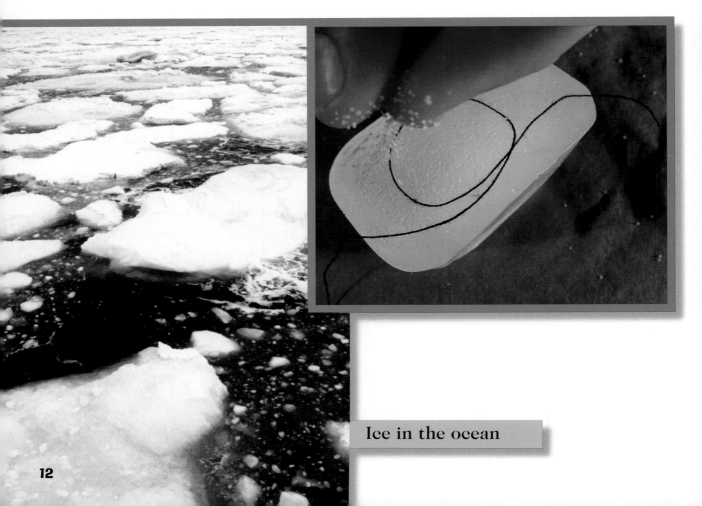

Ice in the ocean

Soon the top of the ice froze once again. Ice formed over the thread and held it in place as you lifted.

Water changes according to its temperature.

Heat water and it evaporates into a gas. Freeze water and it turns to ice.

13

All Mixed Up?
No!

Water and oil will have nothing to do with one another!

Too tiny to see with just your eyes, the **molecules** of oil and water are to blame.

Like you, water and oil are made of molecules.

The molecules in water stick together like these metal balls.

The molecules in oil spread out evenly like these clay balls.

What happens when you put them together?

The Storm

What You Need:
- A clear vase that can hold four cups of liquid
- 2 cups water
- Food coloring
- 1 cup cooking oil
- 1/2 cup salt
- A tablespoon

16

Add a drop of coloring to the water.

Pour the water in the vase.

Pour in the oil.

Why does the water end up on the bottom?

Water is more **dense** than oil. Water molecules are much smaller than oil molecules and pack more tightly together.

It's like putting tiny metal balls and big clay balls in a jar. All the metal balls will fall to the bottom.

Dump in a few
spoonfuls of salt.

Watch what happens.

Urp!

19

Why?

Salt sinks, bringing oil with it. Then the salt **dissolves** in the water, freeing the oil.

The water molecules won't mix with the oil molecules. The oil bubbles back up!

What Are You Made of?

More than half of your body is made up of salt water. You get water by drinking, eating foods that contain liquid, and by breathing water vapor in air.

Unlike oil and water, you and water have everything to do with each other!

Glossary

dense (dens) — crowded closely together, compact

dissolves (dih ZOLVZ) — melts into something

evaporate (ih VAP uh rayt) — change into vapor

gas (GAS) — tiny bits of matter that will fill a
   container and can spread apart without end

molecules (MOL eh kyoolz) — the smallest whole
   part of matter

solid (SOL id) — matter that is firm and has a shape

temperature (TEM per uh cher) — A measurement
   of hot and cold

water vapor (WA ter VAY per) — Water when it is
   a gas

Take It Further: Wave Bottle

- Add a drop of blue food coloring to 1 cup of water.

- Using a funnel, pour the colored water into a 1 pint (500 mL) bottle.

- Use the funnel to pour 1 cup of baby oil into the bottle.

- Put the cap on the bottle

- Wrap duct tape around the bottom of the bottlecap where it covers the bottle.

- Gently tilt the bottle to and fro.

- Watch the waves!

Think About It!

1. When roads get covered in ice, road crews put salt on the ice. Why?

2. What happens to oil that spills in the ocean?

3. Which happens first, second, and third?
   a. Water evaporates
   b. The sun warms the water
   c. You write your name with water

Index